Pitch and Rhythm
Treble Clef
Diatonic
Assorted Meters

Pitch and Rhythm – Treble Clef – Diatonic – Assorted Meters by Nathan Petitpas, published by Dots and Beams, Toronto, Ontario, Canada.

©2019 Nathan Petitpas, Dots and Beams. All rights reserved.

No portion of this book may be copied or redistributed without the permission of the publisher

ISBN 978-1-9990356-0-0

www.DotsandBeams.com

Contents

Introductions:

    About Dots and Beams..1

    About the Author..1

    Preface: How To Use This Book...2

Exercises:

    Chapter 1: Difficulty Level 1..3

    Chapter 2: Difficulty Level 2...16

    Chapter 3: Difficulty Level 3...29

    Chapter 4: Difficulty Level 4...42

    Chapter 5: Difficulty Level 5...55

    Chapter 6: Difficulty Level 6...68

    Chapter 7: Difficulty Level 7...81

    Chapter 8: Difficulty Level 8...94

    Chapter 9: Difficulty Level 9..107

About Dots and Beams

Have you ever created a musical exercise, for yourself or for a student, that would have been much more effective if you could just find a few pages of a certain type of reading material? Perhaps you're a drummer looking for pages of rhythms for developing your timing or coordination. Or maybe you're a pianist looking for melodic reading material to play in your right hand to help develop coordination with a difficult ostinato or bass line. Perhaps you're an experienced musician learning a second instrument; you may feel you would benefit from pages of random notes on a staff to help you become familiar with your new instrument. Or maybe you'd like to mix up your scale practice by playing your scales in unpredictable rhythms rather than the patterns you have been using for years. Maybe you've always played guitar by ear and have lately been wanting to learn to read music; you might want something graduated and systematic to read to help you learn the elements of musical notation but you don't want to play nursery rhymes.

Dots and Beams was created to provide a wide variety of reading materials for musicians at all skill levels and for all instruments.

My approach to creating reading material is slightly different from other approaches I've seen. Many other sight-reading books provide a series of musical compositions for use in practising sight-reading. Rather than provide books of compositions, my approach is to break down the language of musical notation into its rhythmic and melodic components and introduce these components to the user in a systematic way.

These pages of notes and rhythms are not intended to be seen as compositions: they do not follow any particular harmonic or melodic structure and the melodies they contain are not repetitive or memorable. They are exercises in which the complexity of the written language of music gradually increases in order to strengthen the user's ability to process the raw data of musical notation. While the Dots and Beams books are an excellent resource to help improve your sight-reading, their unique construction ensures that the additional uses for these books are as varied and individual as the musicians using them.

Each book in the Dots and Beams collection focuses on a specific element of musical notation. This ensures that you always have the perfect reading material for any exercise so that you can isolate the specific areas in your playing that you feel you need to work on. These books offer very little in the way of explanation and descriptions in an effort to provide as much note-reading material as possible. This is not so much a method book as it is a tool to help make practice more focused and effective.

My hope is that this collection will be one that you will revisit year after year as you find newer, more creative, and more challenging ways to use the materials to push your playing, and your students' playing, to new levels.

About the Author

Nathan Petitpas is a percussionist living in Toronto, Ontario, Canada. He works predominantly as a freelancer in the Ontario orchestra scene as well as the Toronto contemporary music scene. He teaches drum set, percussion, music theory, and general music classes in a variety of programs across Toronto. Nathan holds a Master of Music degree from the University of Toronto and a Bachelor of Music degree from Acadia University, both with a concentration in percussion performance.

Preface: How To Use This Book

This collection presents its user with a series of notes on a treble staff in the context of increasingly complex rhythmic material.

The pitch material in this book is entirely diatonic with a space left at the beginning of each system in which one can write a key signature. Early chapters use only notes on the staff while subsequent chapters begin to add notes on ledger lines above and below the staff. Each chapter contains two exercises in each of the following time signatures: 2/4, 3/4, 4/4, 6/8, 9/8, and 12/8. This gives exercises in 2, 3, and 4 beats per bar in both simple and compound meters. From chapter to chapter the conceptual difficulty of the rhythmic material increases.

The exercises in this collection are intentionally aimless, wandering, and difficult to internalize. They resemble standard melodies on the surface but don't emphasize any particular tonal centre or harmonic movement. They are designed this way for several reasons.

In keeping the melodic material as non-specific as possible the door is left open for the materials to be used in conjunction with any number of exercises, something that would be much more difficult with a composition that dictates the harmonic, melodic, and rhythmic phrasing. It also allows the user to read the exercises in any key signature, making this a great tool to help students learn to think in different keys. The unpredictability of these exercises also forces the user to process every note and rhythm as its own event without relying on pattern recognition or melodic and harmonic tendencies to help in figuring out the notes and rhythms.

While I absolutely agree that the skill of predicting music's direction from harmonic and melodic cues is an essential skill for any musician to develop, I think we will all agree that resources for this type of reading practice are already abundant. This collection, on the other hand, is designed to develop the user's ability to process raw musical data. Once this skill is strengthened and internalized it is my belief that the act of reading more predictable and typically melodic music will be made much easier as the processing of notes and rhythms will be second nature, allowing the musician to focus on musicality. This book is a supplement to practising sight-reading using "real music," not a replacement; I encourage you to use both.

If this material is being used to practice sight-reading, it is encouraged to cycle through the exercises quickly rather than dwelling on a particular exercise for a long period of time. The goal in practising sight-reading is not to learn the material but to develop the skill of reading new material.

Some suggestions for how to use this book include:

- Read each exercise in all 15 key signatures from 7 flats to 7 sharps.
- Practice key changes by writing in a different key signature for each system.
- Increase the challenge of the previous exercise by using a metronome on weak beats. For example, instead of putting the metronome click on each quarter-note in 4/4, play the exercise with the metronome giving the second eighth note of each beat, or the last sixteenth note, or beats 2 and 4. Be creative with this one, the possibilities are limitless.
- Develop independence between hands by playing a repeating pattern in one hand while reading an exercise in the other.
- Write in articulations, dynamics, bowing, sticking, or fingering for your students to practice.

As with any of the Dots and Beams books, the uses for this particular collection are limited only by the imagination of the musician using it. I highly encourage anybody using this book to find as many uses for these exercises as possible.

Chapter 1:

Difficulty Level 1

Difficulty Level 1
Exercise 1 (2/4 Time)

www.DotsandBeams.com

Difficulty Level 1
Exercise 2 (2/4 Time)

www.DotsandBeams.com

Difficulty Level 1
Exercise 3 (3/4 Time)

www.DotsandBeams.com

Difficulty Level 1
Exercise 4 (3/4 Time)

www.DotsandBeams.com

Difficulty Level 1
Exercise 6 (4/4 Time)

www.DotsandBeams.com

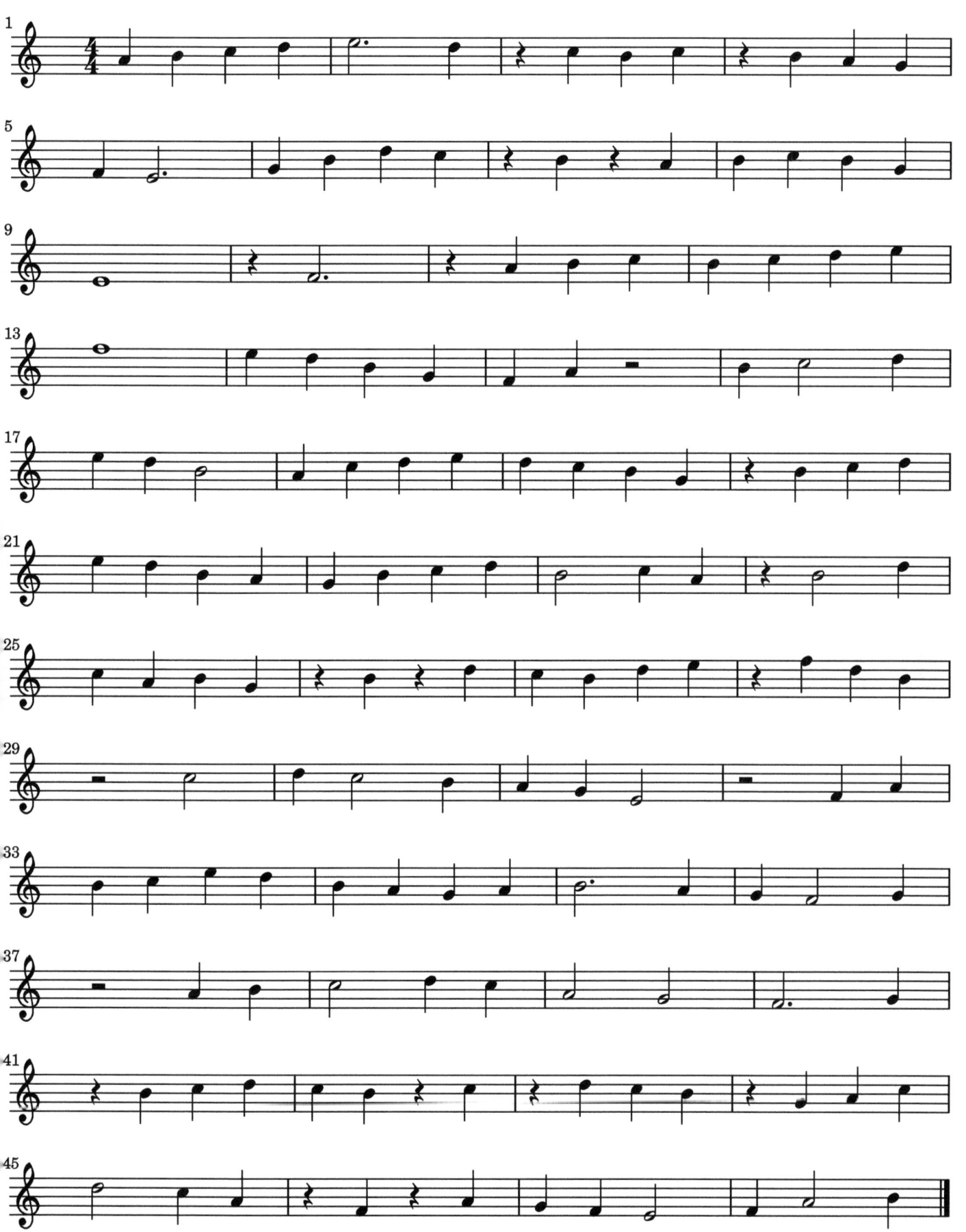

Difficulty Level 1
Exercise 7 (6/8 Time)

www.DotsandBeams.com

Difficulty Level 1
Exercise 8 (6/8 Time)

www.DotsandBeams.com

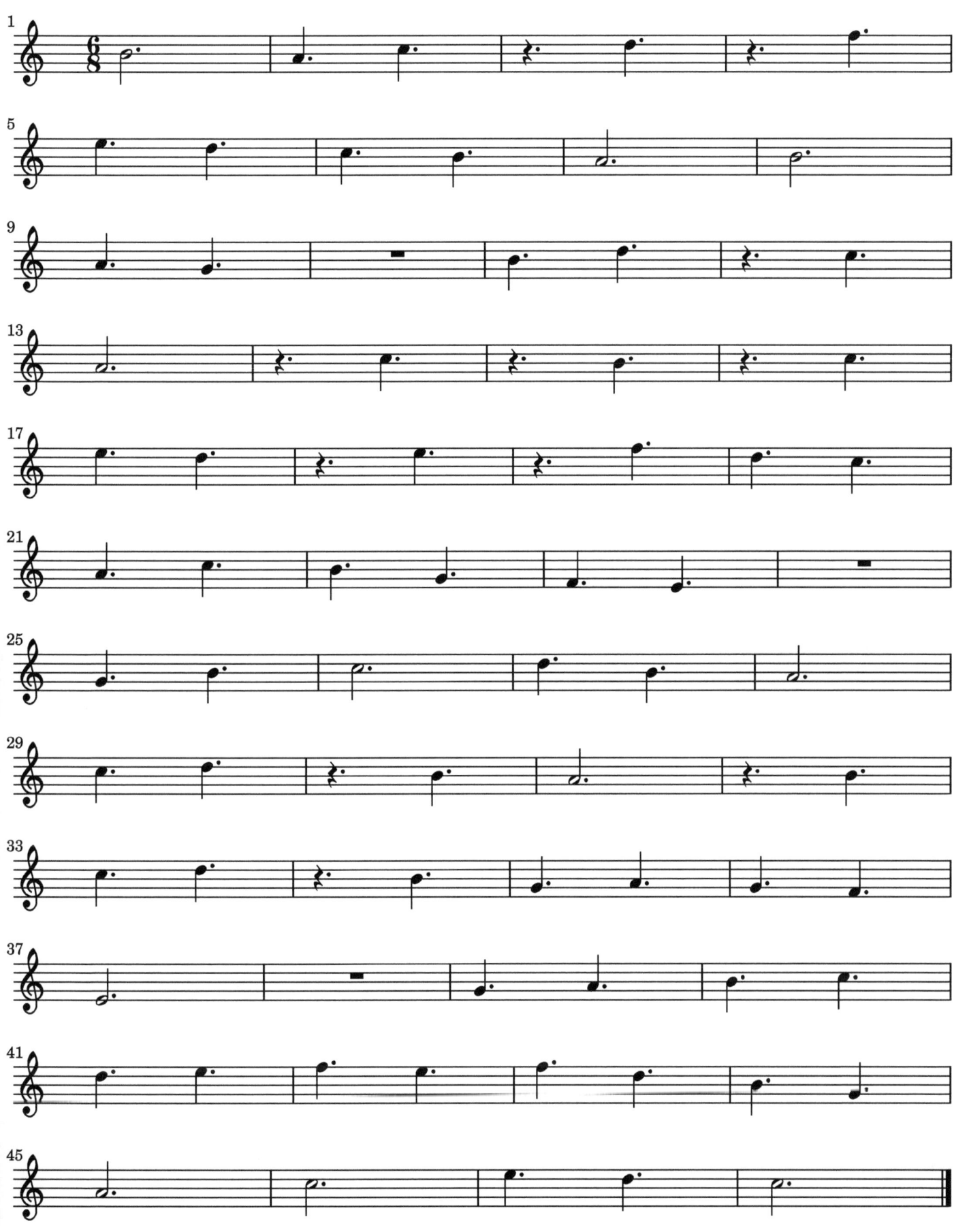

Difficulty Level 1
Exercise 9 (9/8 Time)

Difficulty Level 1
Exercise 10 (9/8 Time)

www.DotsandBeams.com

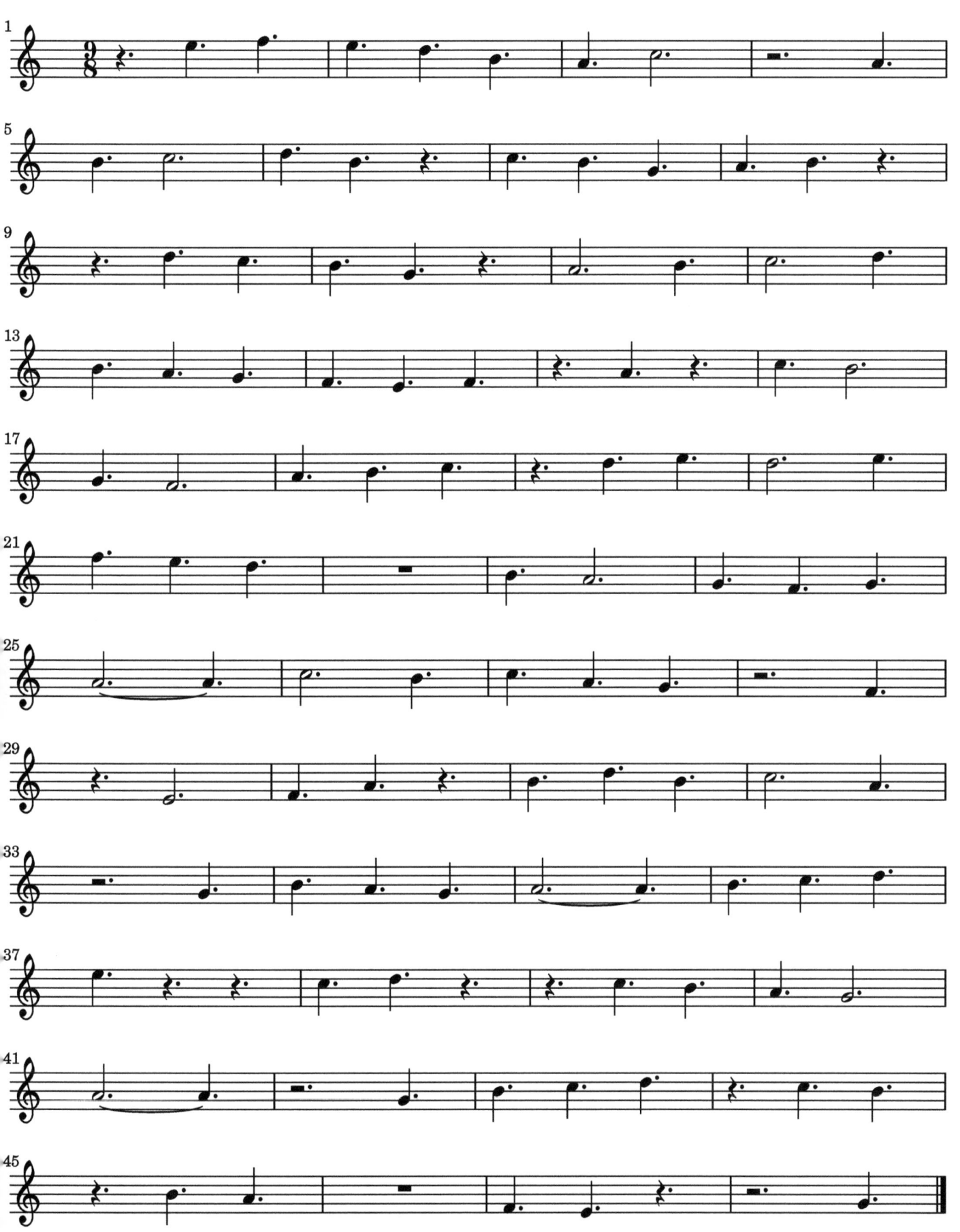

13

Difficulty Level 1
Exercise 11 (12/8 Time)

Difficulty Level 1
Exercise 12 (12/8 Time)

www.DotsandBeams.com

Chapter 2:

Difficulty Level 2

Difficulty Level 2
Exercise 1 (2/4 Time)

www.DotsandBeams.com

Difficulty Level 2
Exercise 2 (2/4 Time)

www.DotsandBeams.com

Difficulty Level 2
Exercise 3 (3/4 Time)

www.DotsandBeams.com

Difficulty Level 2
Exercise 4 (3/4 Time)

Difficulty Level 2
Exercise 5 (4/4 Time)

www.DotsandBeams.com

Difficulty Level 2
Exercise 6 (4/4 Time)

www.DotsandBeams.com

Difficulty Level 2
Exercise 7 (6/8 Time)

www.DotsandBeams.com

Difficulty Level 2
Exercise 8 (6/8 Time)

Difficulty Level 2
Exercise 9 (9/8 Time)

www.DotsandBeams.com

Difficulty Level 2
Exercise 10 (9/8 Time)

Difficulty Level 2
Exercise 11 (12/8 Time)

www.DotsandBeams.com

Difficulty Level 2
Exercise 12 (12/8 Time)

www.DotsandBeams.com

Chapter 3:

Difficulty Level 3

Difficulty Level 3
Exercise 1 (2/4 Time)

www.DotsandBeams.com

Difficulty Level 3
Exercise 2 (2/4 Time)

www.DotsandBeams.com

Difficulty Level 3
Exercise 3 (3/4 Time)

www.DotsandBeams.com

Difficulty Level 3
Exercise 4 (3/4 Time)

www.DotsandBeams.com

Difficulty Level 3
Exercise 5 (4/4 Time)

www.DotsandBeams.com

Difficulty Level 3
Exercise 6 (4/4 Time)

www.DotsandBeams.com

Difficulty Level 3
Exercise 7 (6/8 Time)

www.DotsandBeams.com

Difficulty Level 3
Exercise 8 (6/8 Time)

www.DotsandBeams.com

Difficulty Level 3
Exercise 9 (9/8 Time)

www.DotsandBeams.com

Difficulty Level 3
Exercise 10 (9/8 Time)

www.DotsandBeams.com

Difficulty Level 3
Exercise 11 (12/8 Time)

www.DotsandBeams.com

Difficulty Level 3
Exercise 12 (12/8 Time)

www.DotsandBeams.com

Chapter 4:

Difficulty Level 4

Difficulty Level 4
Exercise 1 (2/4 Time)

www.DotsandBeams.com

Difficulty Level 4
Exercise 2 (2/4 Time)

www.DotsandBeams.com

Difficulty Level 4
Exercise 3 (3/4 Time)

www.DotsandBeams.com

Difficulty Level 4
Exercise 4 (3/4 Time)

www.DotsandBeams.com

Difficulty Level 4
Exercise 5 (4/4 Time)

www.DotsandBeams.com

Difficulty Level 4
Exercise 6 (4/4 Time)

www.DotsandBeams.com

Difficulty Level 4
Exercise 7 (6/8 Time)

www.DotsandBeams.com

Difficulty Level 4
Exercise 8 (6/8 Time)

Difficulty Level 4
Exercise 9 (9/8 Time)

www.DotsandBeams.com

Difficulty Level 4
Exercise 10 (9/8 Time)

Difficulty Level 4
Exercise 11 (12/8 Time)

www.DotsandBeams.com

Difficulty Level 4
Exercise 12 (12/8 Time)

www.DotsandBeams.com

Chapter 5:

Difficulty Level 5

Difficulty Level 5
Exercise 1 (2/4 Time)

www.DotsandBeams.com

Difficulty Level 5
Exercise 2 (2/4 Time)

www.DotsandBeams.com

57

Difficulty Level 5
Exercise 3 (3/4 Time)

www.DotsandBeams.com

Difficulty Level 5
Exercise 4 (3/4 Time)

www.DotsandBeams.com

Difficulty Level 5
Exercise 5 (4/4 Time)

www.DotsandBeams.com

Difficulty Level 5
Exercise 6 (4/4 Time)

www.DotsandBeams.com

Difficulty Level 5
Exercise 7 (6/8 Time)

www.DotsandBeams.com

Difficulty Level 5
Exercise 8 (6/8 Time)

www.DotsandBeams.com

Difficulty Level 5
Exercise 9 (9/8 Time)

www.DotsandBeams.com

Difficulty Level 5
Exercise 10 (9/8 Time)

www.DotsandBeams.com

Difficulty Level 5
Exercise 11 (12/8 Time)

www.DotsandBeams.com

Difficulty Level 5
Exercise 12 (12/8 Time)

www.DotsandBeams.com

Chapter 6:

Difficulty Level 6

Difficulty Level 6
Exercise 1 (2/4 Time)

www.DotsandBeams.com

Difficulty Level 6
Exercise 2 (2/4 Time)

www.DotsandBeams.com

Difficulty Level 6
Exercise 3 (3/4 Time)

www.DotsandBeams.com

Difficulty Level 6
Exercise 4 (3/4 Time)

Difficulty Level 6
Exercise 5 (4/4 Time)

www.DotsandBeams.com

Difficulty Level 6
Exercise 6 (4/4 Time)

www.DotsandBeams.com

Difficulty Level 6
Exercise 7 (6/8 Time)

www.DotsandBeams.com

Difficulty Level 6
Exercise 8 (6/8 Time)

www.DotsandBeams.com

Difficulty Level 6
Exercise 9 (9/8 Time)

www.DotsandBeams.com

Difficulty Level 6
Exercise 10 (9/8 Time)

www.DotsandBeams.com

Difficulty Level 6
Exercise 11 (12/8 Time)

www.DotsandBeams.com

Difficulty Level 6
Exercise 12 (12/8 Time)

www.DotsandBeams.com

Chapter 7:

Difficulty Level 7

Difficulty Level 7
Exercise 1 (2/4 Time)

www.DotsandBeams.com

Difficulty Level 7
Exercise 2 (2/4 Time)

www.DotsandBeams.com

Difficulty Level 7
Exercise 3 (3/4 Time)

www.DotsandBeams.com

Difficulty Level 7
Exercise 4 (3/4 Time)

www.DotsandBeams.com

Difficulty Level 7
Exercise 5 (4/4 Time)

www.DotsandBeams.com

Difficulty Level 7
Exercise 6 (4/4 Time)

www.DotsandBeams.com

Difficulty Level 7
Exercise 7 (6/8 Time)

www.DotsandBeams.com

Difficulty Level 7
Exercise 8 (6/8 Time)

www.DotsandBeams.com

Difficulty Level 7
Exercise 9 (9/8 Time)

www.DotsandBeams.com

Difficulty Level 7
Exercise 10 (9/8 Time)

www.DotsandBeams.com

Difficulty Level 7
Exercise 11 (12/8 Time)

www.DotsandBeams.com

Difficulty Level 7
Exercise 12 (12/8 Time)

www.DotsandBeams.com

Chapter 8:

Difficulty Level 8

Difficulty Level 8
Exercise 1 (2/4 Time)

www.DotsandBeams.com

Difficulty Level 8
Exercise 2 (2/4 Time)

www.DotsandBeams.com

Difficulty Level 8
Exercise 3 (3/4 Time)

www.DotsandBeams.com

Difficulty Level 8
Exercise 4 (3/4 Time)

www.DotsandBeams.com

Difficulty Level 8
Exercise 5 (4/4 Time)

Difficulty Level 8
Exercise 6 (4/4 Time)

www.DotsandBeams.com

Difficulty Level 8
Exercise 7 (6/8 Time)

www.DotsandBeams.com

Difficulty Level 8
Exercise 8 (6/8 Time)

www.DotsandBeams.com

Difficulty Level 8
Exercise 9 (9/8 Time)

www.DotsandBeams.com

Difficulty Level 8
Exercise 10 (9/8 Time)

www.DotsandBeams.com

Difficulty Level 8
Exercise 11 (12/8 Time)

www.DotsandBeams.com

Difficulty Level 8
Exercise 12 (12/8 Time)

www.DotsandBeams.com

Chapter 9:

Difficulty Level 9

Difficulty Level 9
Exercise 2 (2/4 Time)

www.DotsandBeams.com

Difficulty Level 9
Exercise 3 (3/4 Time)

www.DotsandBeams.com

Difficulty Level 9
Exercise 4 (3/4 Time)

Difficulty Level 9
Exercise 6 (4/4 Time)

www.DotsandBeams.com

Difficulty Level 9
Exercise 7 (6/8 Time)

www.DotsandBeams.com

Difficulty Level 9
Exercise 8 (6/8 Time)

www.DotsandBeams.com

Difficulty Level 9
Exercise 9 (9/8 Time)

www.DotsandBeams.com

Difficulty Level 9
Exercise 10 (9/8 Time)

www.DotsandBeams.com

Difficulty Level 9
Exercise 12 (12/8 Time)

www.DotsandBeams.com

Thank You!

For more materials please visit
www.DotsandBeams.com

Milton Keynes UK
Ingram Content Group UK Ltd.
UKHW020728260324
440002UK00004B/140